The Heart of a Woman

The Heart of a Woman

The Depth of Her Spirit

The Heart of a Woman

The Heart of a Woman

The Depth of Her Spirit

By
Onedia N. Gage, CLC, Ph. D.

The Heart of a Woman

The Depth of Her Spirit

Other Books by Onedia N. Gage, Ph. D.

Are You Ready for 9th Grade . . . Again? A Family's Guide to Success
As We Grow Together Daily Devotional for Expectant Couples
As We Grow Together Prayer Journal for Expectant Couples
As We Grow Together Bible Study: Her Workbook
As We Grow Together Bible Study: His Workbook
The Best 40 Days of My Life: A Journey of Spiritual Renewal
The Blue Print: Poetry for the Soul
From Fat to Fit in 90 Days: A Fitness Journal
From Two to One: The Notebook for the Christian Couple
Hannah's Voice: Powerful Lessons in Prayer
Her Story The Legacy of Her Fight: The Bible Study
Her Story The Legacy of Her Fight: The Devotional
Her Story The Legacy of Her Fight: The Legacy Journal
Her Story The Legacy of Her Fight: Prayers and Journal
I Am.: 90 Days of Powerful Words: Affirmation and Advice for Girls
ILY! A Mother Daughter Relationship Workbook
In Her Own Words: Notebook for the Christian Woman
In 90 Days: What Will You Do?
In Purple Ink: Poetry for the Spirit
In Your Hands: A Dad's Impact on Your Daughter's Self-Esteem
Intensive Couples Retreat: Her Workbook
Intensive Couples Retreat: His Workbook
Living A Whole Life: Sermons Which Prompt, Provoke and Provide Life
Love Letters to God from a Teenage Girl
The Measure of a Woman: The Details of Her Soul
The Notebook: For Me, About Me, By Me
The Notebook for the Christian Teen
On This Journey Daily Devotional for Young People
On This Journey Prayer Journal for Young People
On This Journey Prayer Journal for Young People, Vol. 2
One Day More Than We Deserve Prayer Journal for the Growing Christian
Promises, Promises: A Novel
Queen in the Making: 30 Week Bible Study for Teen Girls
Queen in the Making: 30 Week Bible Study for Teen Girls Leader's Guide
There's a Queen Within: Her Journey to Self—Worth
She Spoke Volumes . . . And Then Some
Six Months of Solitude: The Sanctity of Singleness Notebook
Six Months of Solitude: The Sanctity of Singleness Prayers and Journal
Tools for These Times: Timely Sermons for Uncertain Times
With An Anointed Voice: The Power of Prayer
A Woman Like Me: A Bible Study

The Heart of a Woman

A Woman Like Me: A Daily Devotional
A Woman Like Me: A Sermonic Study
Yielded and Submitted: A Woman's Journey for a Life Dedicated to God
Yielded and Submitted: A Woman's Journey for a Life Dedicated to God An Intimate Study
Yielded and Submitted: A Woman's Journey for a Life Dedicated to God Prayers and Journal

The Nehemiah Character Series

Nehemiah and His Basketball
Nehemiah and His Big Sister
Nehemiah and His Bike
Nehemiah and His Flag Football Team
Nehemiah and His Football
Nehemiah and His Golf Clubs
Nehemiah and Math
Nehemiah and the Bully
Nehemiah and the Busy Day
Nehemiah and the Class Field Trip
Nehemiah and the Substitute for the Substitute
Nehemiah Can Swim
Nehemiah Found the Mud
Nehemiah Reads to Mommy
Nehemiah Writes Just Like Mommy
Nehemiah, the Hot Dog, and the Broccoli
Nehemiah's Family Vacation
Nehemiah's Favorite Teacher Returns to School
Nehemiah's First Day of School
Nehemiah's Sister Moved
Nehemiah's Visit to the Hospital

Dedication

Women with a broken heart.

Women with a bountiful heart.

Women with a beautiful heart.

And those who love her and want to study her.

Library of Congress

The Heart of a Woman:

The Depth of Her Spirit

All Rights Reserved © 2021

Onedia N. Gage, Ph. D.

No part of this of book may be reproduced or transmitted in
Any form or by any means, graphic, electronic, or mechanical,
Including photocopying, recording, taping, or by any
Information storage or retrieval system, without the
Permission in writing from the publisher.

Purple Ink, Inc. Press
For Information address:
Purple Ink, Inc
10223 Broadway St., Ste. P292
Houston, TX 77584
www.purpleink.net ♦ www.onediagage.com

onediagage@purpleink.net ♦ onediagage@onediagage.com

ISBN:

978-1-939119-12-4

Printed in United States

What God Has to Say

Come unto me, all ye that labour and are heavy laden, and I will give you rest.

> Matthew 11:28 (KJV)

For where your treasure is, there your heart will be also.

> Matthew 6:21

[16] I pray that out of his glorious riches he may strengthen you with power through his Spirit in your inner being, [17] so that Christ may dwell in your hearts through faith. And I pray that you, being rooted and established in love, [18] may have power, together with all the Lord's holy people, to grasp how wide and long and high and deep is the love of Christ,

> Ephesians 3:16—18

The Heart of a Woman

The Depth of Her Spirit

Dear God,

I pray You bless me. I know that my silence in this season has its issues, however I am devastated about how my life is progressing. The need for this study comes at a time when I need affirmation and other women like me need the same. WE need to hear from You. WE need to see Your hand of protection over our lives and that of our families. WE need a miracle in our careers and finances. We have dreams and goals that we need to see to develop and materialize.

WE need to be able to see the realization of our prayers. WE need to have what we pray for and be the women You have called for and make sure that we are able to testify to that fact that You are the God that we pray to and attest to and worship to and witness about. WE need something new to witness about.

I pray that You bless the women will read, share and be blessed and spiritually fed from this study. I labored and was uplifted. I toiled and was replenished. I whined and You offered me some grace. I wept and You sent me a shoulder. I studied and You gave me a retreat.

The Heart of a Woman

Lord, I am questioning the lessons and the outcome. I am considering the world and our current situation. We are under the attack of disease. What message are You sending? What do You want from us? What do You want us to do now?

Lord, thank You for entrusting me with this book, these words, and this study. I pray that I listen to Your voice to share the correct words that You want seen. Lord, thank You for using me! Lord, I so want to impress You by obeying You!

I pray for these blessings in Jesus' name.

Amen.

The Depth of Her Spirit

Dear Woman With a Heart:

I know that you are like me in many ways and that is SCARY. I am certainly on edge, in a bad head space, need to hear from the God who declared His love for me, but I cannot see it because I need it to look like something else. As a woman, we have many roles and jobs, desires and dreams, however we will only achieve those to which He consents. I am certain that He heard me but He tells me no or wait. At some point, He tells me yes and then we may be in real trouble. So if you are really like me, we are dangerous and in trouble.

With that in mind, we need to heal. My prayer is that your healing is instrumental and inspirational to others whose paths you will cross. In the meantime, as you read these works, I hope that you also allow these words to minister to you so that you are whole emotionally and spiritually—better than ever before.

One of my favorite Bible verses is 1 Corinthians 13:13, the Message version, which reads: "Love extravagantly." This is a great time for you to remove the boundaries of your love and love outrageously with an understanding that you can NEVER run out. You are not the supplier of your own love. God is. Love because He loves you.

Further, love heals. In this love and healing, you can overcome. Use this time to heal from everything.

The Heart of a Woman

Leave a HUGE legacy! Start with yourself!!

I look forward to hearing from you. Feel free to share with me as you journey. You can follow me on twitter @onediangage, email onediagage@onediagage.com, facebook.com/onediagageministries, blogtalkradio.com/onediagage, and youtube.com/onediagage. www.onediagage.com

I can hardly wait!

Onedia N Gage

Onedia N. Gage, Ph. D.

Table of Contents

Prayer   15

Letters   17

Poem: "The Measure of a Woman"   25

The Heart of a Woman   27

Acknowledgements   215

About the Woman   217

The Heart of a Woman

The Measure of a Woman

By Onedia N. Gage

The Measure of a Woman

    What is the width of her spirit

    What is the depth of her mind

    What is the weight of her heart

    What is the volume of her body

    What is the capacity of her mind

    What is the speed of her thoughts

    What is the circumference of her hugs

    What is the breadth of her love

    How many inches does she let you within the boundaries of her heart

    How many feet until she reaches forgiveness

    What is the slope of her attitude

    What is the velocity of her meekness

The Measure of a Woman

The Heart of a Woman

>She thinks critically
>
>She plans carefully
>
>She speaks dynamically
>
>She loves passionately
>
>She lives authentically
>
>She moves fearlessly
>
>She leads humbly
>
>She fears God

Experience the Measure of a Woman

>Her love
>
>Her fears
>
>Her tears
>
>Her victories
>
>Her power
>
>Her influence
>
>Her motivation

Invest in the Measure of a Woman

The Depth of Her Spirit

Create for her a loving environment

Create for her a safe place

Go the distance for the Measure of a Woman

The Measure of a Woman

    Defines love

    Defies opposition

    Declares independence

    Decorates hearts

    Demands chemistry

The Measure of a Woman

Reprinted from <u>The Measure of a Woman: The Details of Her Soul</u>

The Heart of a Woman

The Heart of a Woman

The Heart of a Woman

There's a Storm in This House

Raging
Rambunctious
Racing
Storm

Uncontrollable
Unequivocable
Unparalleled
Storm

Outlandish
Outrageous
Overwhelming
Storm

Undeniable
Un—relinquishing
Unique
Storm

Pressure Filled
Powerful
Perfect
Storm

The Heart of a Woman

There's a Storm in This House
What is the measure of the Storm
Size
Speed
Wind
Category

Is the Storm always in season or does it have limits?

How much damage will this Storm cause?
How much damage has It caused already?
Will this house fall?
Total obliteration?

There is a storm in this house.
Can you survive the Storm?
The Calm before its rampage?
And all It's torrential rain?
The magnitude of the damage?
The after math of the storm?
Will the house stand?
There is indeed a storm in this house.

6/16/20

An Intimate Release

A release

An escape

A heightened awareness

Sensual moments

Warm conversation

Holding hands

Touch unparalleled experience

Glances unknown path

Breaths curious resistance

    Short

    Heavy

Fingertips

Lips

Whispers

Hungry grasp

Exploratory tongue

Holding your breath

The Heart of a Woman

Taken to the place where intimacy breeds
Elevated to the intimate level one only dreams
Resulting in an intimate release
Beyond measure

6/16/20

The Depth of Her Spirit

When Their Eyes Meet

The things that happen
When your eyes meet with somebody else's
From across the room are limitless

The eye and mind combine to form imagination
The eye and the mind's imagination

What do you do when your eyes meet?
What do you when you are excited or blush?
Could it be that you are embarrassed to get caught?

Do you think?
Do you dream?
Do you hope?
Do you wonder?
Does your mind wander?

Does that glance mean something?
Or do you hope that it will?

Their eyes meet.
Their minds race.

The Heart of a Woman

Their hearts flutter.
Their temperatures rise.
Their imaginations start.

When their eyes meet
    They have a chance to change their course
    They can change their path
    And the path of the other person

When their eyes meet
    Chemistry stirs
    Energy develops
    Compatibility tested
    Tensions rise
    Fears dissipate

What are you going to do
    When your eyes meet?

When your eyes meet.

6/23/2020

Surrender

Roadblocks

Obstacles

And fort knox

Make love impossible

Some of that is self—sabotage

You built that wall

Yet you posted a sign

"love wanted here"

"Love welcome here"

"Love needed here"

But why would you

Why would hang that sign

You had no intention of love

Or loving

Or being loved

But you want to

Or so you think

Then let down the wall

Be ready for the fort to be stormed

Let the draw bridge down

Let her cross that moat

The Heart of a Woman

Into the castle

An act of surrender

Wave the white flag

Wave the white flag

Throw in the towel

Tap out

Quit

Surrender

    Total

    Completely

Succumb to love

Succumb to your lover

Surrender to love

You wanted it

You needed it

Your craved it

You sought it

You solicited it

You actually campaigned for it

And championed it

But you can't relinquish to it

Surrender

You won't know love until you surrender to it

Love or let go.

6/15/20

The Heart of a Woman

The Perfect Circle of Love

A perfectly round circle

No breaks

No seams

No flaws

No beginning

And definitely, no end

A circle—perfectly round

A radius

A diameter

A circumference

Exact numerical measurements

A perfect circle of love

An impenetrable union

A complete partnership

One that no man can put asunder

A great team

Boy meets girl

Girl likes boy

Boy asks girl to dance

The Depth of Her Spirit

Girl says yes

Girl kisses boy

Boy loves girl

Girl loves boy in return

Boy pledges his love and life to her

Girl pledges as well

The circle they form

    Perfect

    Passionate

    Committed

    Complete

    Comprehensive

    Compound

    Unique

Perfect Circle of Love

For Them

6/14/20

The Heart of a Woman

An In Spite of Love

How do you define love
By actions
Not so much by words
How do you measure love
By time spent
Not thoughts

How do you show love
By deeds
Not broken promises

How do you overcome love's obstacles
By communication
Rather than arguing

How do you have an authentic love
By investment
Not by neglect

How do you achieve a love which stands the test of time
By never quitting
By never giving up

How do you build an 'in spite of love'
The love which lasts past the fights

The Depth of Her Spirit

The love which endures the many storms

The love which creates a whole bond between the two lovers

The love which overcomes obstacles

The love which meets the needs of the other mate

The love which still loves during an argument

The love which affirms you, upholds you, and keeps you whole

The love which keeps you close

The love which builds your strength and self-esteem

The love which fights through to the eternity

How do you build an in spite of love

In spite of hurt

> Pain
>
> Disappointment
>
> Death
>
> Disdain
>
> Disagreements
>
> Differences

An in spite of love that overcomes all that is designed to tear the relationship apart.

06/14/20

The Heart of a Woman

A Partner's Heart

Melts the Heart

Holds the Heart

Softens the Heart

Allows the potter in and within

Take care of your partner's heart.

06/14/20

The Depth of Her Spirit

See and Don't See

There's a whole lot more to me
Than what you see

I always hated iceberg metaphor
And the picture of it
    —so much beneath the surface
    —so little above

So little that you see
Or that you question
And that you understand

You want to know what you don't know
I know this because
You are amazed at what comes out of my mouth
Out of my mind
And from my journals

Some of it a secret
Some no longer relevant
Part too personal to share
The rest too important to reveal

Not exactly transparent
But revealing

The Heart of a Woman

Exposed on paper

Shared in person

Active in media

Not transparent

But open

Open to questions

Open to probing

Open to sharing

There's more

A whole lot more

Of me

Than what you can see with the naked eye

A bit of advice

Use your heart to know

Employ your mind to seek

Explore with your soul to extract details of me

How much more do you want to know of the whole lot

More there is

Of me?

6/14/20

Am I Asking for the Right Things?

In the quietness of my soul
In the depth of my spirit
Am I seeking the right things

In the crevices of my mind
In the breadth of my heart
Am I passionate about the right stuff

In the recess of my secret places
In the spirit of excellence
Am I working in the right direction

What do I want?
What do I need?
What can I have?
What can't I?

Why can't I have what I want?
When will I get it
—at least part of it
—some of it
—just one piece

The Heart of a Woman

—if not all

I mean I really need what I asked for
I really do.

6/14/20

The Depth of Her Spirit

A Mile in My Moccasins

Where I have been

Where I am

Where I am going

What does my journey mean

The pain

    The power

The promise

    The presence

The extreme measures

    The over-achievement

The questions

    The inquisitions

The answers

    The acquisition

The reasons

    The strategy

The strength

    The struggle

The energy

    The chemistry

The fierce

The Heart of a Woman

        The outlandish

The outrageous

        The pleasure

The journey

        These miles

        Speak of happiness and joy

Share triumph and victory

Strip pain and agony

Swallow hopelessness and helplessness

Sabotage enemies and unfavorable elements

Show peace and patience

Spark inspiration and motivation

Shout outlandish and outrageous

Spend compassion and empathy

These days and distance

Dictate how you see me

Delegate what you think of me

Decide how my life will proceed

Determine what I will achieve

Defines the power of my dash

Details the distress of those events

Distances the competition

Defeats the nay-sayers

The Depth of Her Spirit

Displaces the fear and anger

A mile in my moccasins is a foot in yours
It's where I have been
Where I am
Where I am going.

06/14/20

The Heart of a Woman

More Than He Could Give

She wanted more than he could give
Or was willing to give
Or was able to offer

She wanted time
But he was too busy

She wanted talks
But he was silent

She wanted walks
But he was massaging the remote

She wanted dates
But he was always late

She wanted companion cooking
But he had to rush out

She wanted to hold hands
But he would not consent

The Depth of Her Spirit

She wanted all of him
But he offered her leftover pieces

She wanted more from the relationship
But he kept her at arm's length

She wanted more than he could give
Now she's disappointed—perpetually.

06/14/20

The Heart of a Woman

Dreams Women Dream

Mrs. Dr. Mom.
At the same time
One at a time

We want it
We want it all
We want it now

We dream
We dream big
Big dreams, we dream

Audacious
Outrageous
Outlandish
Ridiculous
Beautiful
Jaw-dropping
    Dreams

Life-changing
Life-altering

Each dream important
Each sought

The Depth of Her Spirit

Fiercely
Fervently
Boldly
Dreams women dream
And dreams which are envied
Struggled for
And strived for
Searched for
And stalked for

Woman, keep dreaming
Keep working for the dreams
The dreams inspire you
Influence you
Keep you sane
Keep you happy, healthy and whole

Woman, keep dreaming
Those dreams keep you breathing
When you would rather quit.

6/14/20

The Heart of a Woman

Feelings

Feelings so deep, so true

Yet unheard, consequently

Unanswered

. . . ultimately unfelt.

06/14/20

A Message to my Love

The hurt and pain takes over my soul's inner peace.

No silence in my mind.

Nor of my body.

I need to feel that warmth,

that passion,

that peace,

that my soul yearns for.

I need you to soothe the pain and tension

Not excite or stimulate the violent emotions

Which run so very deep.

Calm the currents in my body that are so highly explosive.

My nature is the strength of heart and mind and soul.

Keep me safe.

Especially from myself.

I want all of the rest of my days to be shared with you.

You inspire me.

You teach me.

You help me.

Your iron sharpens mine.

The Heart of a Woman

You love me.

You invoke a response from me.

My love.

My heart.

6/14/20

Deserved

If you leave your money on the table, then you will return to nothing.

As it is in relationships.

If it were valuable, you would have never left if unprotected.

So now that it's gone, why are you in search of it?

Did you not want it?

Did something change that made you leave it unprotected?

Do you want it—the relationship?

Why now?

Or did you not intend for this to go this far?

Do you value it now?

What happened?

How did you invest in the relationship if you had no intention of maintaining that same relationship?

Your partner deserves what you promised her and you deserve what she promised you.

Life's brevity demands an outlandish course of action

Do it big

Make the grand gesture

Splurge on the details

Open your mind

The Heart of a Woman

Unlock your heart

Abandon your fears

Stop listening to the noise which causes you to change your relational direction

You went looking for companion

But you can't give her all that she needs.

Give her what she deserves

What she needs

What she desires

Deserved.

06/13/20

The Depth of Her Spirit

The Layers

The blue print was in layers
Which layer did you show?

First is the elevation
The front of the house
The beauty of it
The fullness of the detail
The texture of the brick and stone and glass

Then there is the electrical layer
The fuel for the house
The power, the air, the heat
      Completely powerful
The power which gives energy to all corners of the house

There is a foundation
How stable is the base
How much weight can the base sustain
How is the foundation built

There is the frame of the house
The pieces that hold the entire house up

The Heart of a Woman

The frame is important

It is the shape of the house

The sheetrock covers

The plumbing

The electrical

The frame

The insulation

The inner workings of the house

The blue print consists of lots of pages

Huge pages

With many details

The blue print reveals the entire house in layers

When you share your blue print

Which layer do you show?

Which layer do you hide?

The layers are important.

06/13/20

In the Singular

For the life of me I cannot figure out why coexistence on this Earth will be summarized as the wife of or never married.

Wonderful it would be if one could establish a life then add a companion and stir.

Imagine no pressure and no accountability.

But is that what you want:

    The singular disposition

Not so much

Because the judgement weighs

An unbearable weight

Thousands of pounds—unmovable weight

You define you

You own that definition

You decide if your marital disposition

Confines to a bound space

And an indescribable time

Either be comfortable

    Or not

Choose to

The Heart of a Woman

        Or not

Confident

        Or not

In the singular

        Or not

06/12/20

Love Is Something . . .

A responsibility	a need
An action	a necessity
A commitment	a challenge
A struggle	a moment
A celebration	a lifetime
A romance	a healer
A memory	a light
A reaction	a solution
A strength	a chance
A response	a change
A miracle	an emotion

Worth working for	worth having
Worth seeking	worth building
Worth searching for	worth investing
Worth taking a stand for	worth risking it all for
Worth giving it all up for	

Love is something that nourishes your soul
And causes your spirit to flourish

Love is something that you don't let go

Love is something . . .

06/13/2020

The Heart of a Woman

Take Me With You

I wanna go
Whenever you are
Close intimate
Proximity

Don't you want me close
Nearby
Within reach
At a glance
So close that I can hear your whispers
And you can hear mine

Take me into your arms
Hold me close
I crave your space
      Your smell
      Your voice
      Your touch

Just to be close to you

I wanna go
I just want to be where you are

06/12/20

What Are We?

In a world of uncertainty

We have discovered one another

Against the odds of

Age

Time

Space

Social media

In a season of discombobulation

We have emotionally collided

Such a discovery

    Exciting

    Exhilarating

    Outrageous

    Outlandish

    Transparent

Fearless

Fierce

Flawless

The Heart of a Woman

Infinite

Bold

Courageous

You met me

I met you

I don't know what we are

Do you?

What are we?

Together?

In a bleak world,

We have sought solace in each other

We define love

And redefine trust

We define joy

And refine intimacy

We defy the social norms

And redefine transparency

We defy boundaries

The Depth of Her Spirit

And redefine longevity

We are outlandish
And completely outrageous!

We are love
And ALL that that means.

Whatever we are, we deserve each other.

06/12/20

The Heart of a Woman

The Taste of My Tears

I can't stand the taste of my tears

Though accustomed to the taste I've become

More and more often they fall in anguish

And grief and pain

Stall the tears

Heal the grief

If I continue the taste my tears

Then I need to walk away.

Tears and love do not co-exist.

06/12/20

A Love Declaration

I hurt and you look at me each day and do or say nothing

I need and you never replenish the love I give

I keep returning to you after you consistently reject me

Your statements are designed to wilt my self—esteem

Yet I still love you and tell you so

I invest in you at an all-in level

But you neglect my simple requests

I am focused on the rest of our lives but you cannot

Let the argument go from yesterday

I want you

I want us

I need you

I need us

I love you

Don't want to live without you

Why should I

I declare

I declare an unrelenting love

The Heart of a Woman

      A powerful union

      A selfless team

      A formidable partner

I declare my love for you

Can you do the same?

06/12/20

The Watering Pot

The pot
> Big base
>
> Waterfall spout
>
> Large handle
>
> Heavy when full

Deposits hydration

Contributes to growth

Cool transfer

Even distribution

The watering pot

Has one job

Water

If it's your turn

To hold the pot

Then do your job

The results

Amazing

Blossoms

Growth

The Heart of a Woman

Extreme measures
Expansion

Sometimes we need the watering pot
Other times we are the watering pot
And then there are times we avoid
The watering pot

06/11/20

The Inside Noise

You are out in the world
You are important; prestigious, even
But you ain't shit when you come home

Not that doctor for which you studied 12 years
Not that elected judge
Not even that licensed therapist

When outside noise sounds better
Than inside
A change should be sought

Peaceful inside noise—I wish
Insightful inside noise—I crave
Respected inside noise—I seek

Outside roles may not influence inside respect
Inside roles should demand inside respect

Dictate the inside noise
Sexy
Respected
Respectful
Loving
Charismatic
Influential
Peaceful
Welcoming

The Heart of a Woman

Pleasant
The inside noise
Should have the power
To bring the outside noise
To its knees
Into an unrelinquishing submission

Crave
Seek
Embellish
Protect
Devote
Influence
The inside noise
    Such that you want it daily
    Without a doubt
        Or reservation
    With love and zeal
    Without hesitation or regret
    While outlandish and outrageous

06/11/20

The Depth of Her Spirit

From Me to You

I must teach you

You must learn

I must show you

You must see

I must tell you

You must know

I must love you

You must love

03/19/1991

The Heart of a Woman

Nobody (Nothing) Like You

Compare
Comparing
Compared
Comparison

To you

What could I measure you against
What could possibly be worth the comparison
Nothing compares to you

Your love
    And its depth

Your care
    And its width

Your sensitivity
    And its value

Your concern
    And its worth

Your investment
    And its rewards

Your companionship
    And its comfort

Your communication
    And its confirmation

All that is incomparable

To others
To another

The Depth of Her Spirit

To things

No
Never
Can't even

Nobody like you

06/11/20

The Heart of a Woman

Loving Others
Loving You

Loving
Loving me
Loving others
Loving you!

Therein lies the difference!

08/07/1994

The Depth of Her Spirit

Life is about the Butterfly on His Bag

Butterflies—such an elusive creature
Wise specimen
Delightful insect
      An insect we like
      Others we crush
Beauty on full display

Tender
Gentle
Strength in its simplicity

On this bag
Its travels
Without destination knowledge
But just an escape
A modality

Teach butterfly teach
Capture opportunities
Seek solutions
Escape space
Demonstrate love
Abandon time

Free flying
Protected
Beautiful
Colorful

Examine life differently
Better even

The Heart of a Woman

Isolate the petal
Specify the exact flower
Explain life fully
Explore life's nuances
One flower at a time

Watch the flight
The flight plan
The height
The speed
The longevity
The beauty
The fullness

The butterfly recognized the escape
Took the risk
Arrived safe
Achieved the goal
Understood the mechanism of escape
    And the route

Life is like that butterfly on that man's bag
    Action met opportunity
    The results were beautiful

06/11/20

Chasing the Sun

Bright
Hot
Romantic
    A sun
    A dream
    A realization

Reality that needs interpretation
A bleak reality
Not great
Escape a broken reality
Pursue the ridiculous—your dreams
    Or desires
The impractical
The unrealistic
The impossible
Unreachable
    Or so it seems
Far-fetched at best
Life is great
So short
No one leaves this life with a completed list
We all leave items on the list

Permission granted
Pursue the irresponsible
Live out loud
Laugh disrespectfully
Be outlandish
Be outrageous

Chase the sun

The Heart of a Woman

You deserve the sun
The sun beckons you

Break the rules
Overcome the obstacles

Chase the sun
        Relentlessly
        Without pause
        Without regret

Chase the sun

06/10/20

The Heart of a Woman

Tender
Compassionate
Humble
Meek
Demure
Protected
Sometimes shy
Warm
Endearing
Affirming
Loving
Forgiving
Energetic
Creative
Inspiring
Loving
Lovable

That heart deserves
love
attention
warmth
challenge
forgiveness
maybe more

what makes her love?
At 100%?
Or less?

What makes her change the path of her love?
What makes her change her mind about love?

The Heart of a Woman

Do you know her heart?
How do you know it?

The heart of a woman
Desires protection from harm
        Especially if that harm is from you
Deserves peace
        Especially from you
Needs care and nurture
        So that she can reciprocate the same
Craves your touch—sensuous and warm
        Provocative and intense
Brokers love
        So that she uses your love to love you and
        Herself and others

The heart of a woman has been
        Bent
        Broken
        Brittle
        Bruised
        Battered
        Bettered
        Blessed
        Blissed
        Brazen
        Bold
        Bankrupt
        Breached
        Bright
        Brilliant

The heart of a woman

The Depth of Her Spirit

Experiences many events and emotions

Keep loving her heart
So that it can heal

And live to love another day.

06/10/20

The Heart of a Woman

Images of Love

The friend you are when I need you and when you need me

Those geese followed their 'mother'
They landed safely
They returned home

You hugged me just before that tear landed on my blouse

When they lowered your body into the ground
I will miss you until it is my turn

That walk—the long one—where I consider how to propose to you
Because forever started a year ago

A simple kiss

When he walked her down the aisle and put her hand in his and took his seat

Water for miles

The birth of children

When the book went live online

The Depth of Her Spirit

When he said I love you to his wife

When she said I love you to her mother

When they took their first vacation together

When he asked her to dance in the restaurant when they first met

He moved her hair from her face so that he could kiss her on her frontal lobe

He pulled her close, into his embrace while snoring—loudly

She cooked dinner from him

He held her hand as she gave birth to their child

He whispered to her before her speech so that she would not be nervous

Those are images of love that makes life worth living.

06/20/20

The Heart of a Woman

Nobody Knows What to Say

Bad news
Sometimes good
Death
Illness
Even joy
Some excitement

But what do I say
What should I say
What to do

Think
Breathe
Think
Consider
Ponder
Reflect
Practice
Practice
Practice
Reflect
Refine
Rehearse

Then present your words . . .
Flawless
Intentional
Stern

The Depth of Her Spirit

Compassionate
Serious
Focused
Wise

Share your words carefully
With care
And understanding
To uplift
To serve
To motivate
To inspire
To reconcile
To forgive
To be forgiven
To solve
To resolve
To fix
To influence
To be

Words have power
Powerfully use them
Use them well and wisely

06/10/20

The Heart of a Woman

Watching Paint Dry

Nothing else to do?
Not so much
Busy to a fault

Life stalled
Life's hiccup
Life hiccupped
An obstacle strutted into your path

No time to watch paint dry
Or to stop the steam engine
Or that race car
Or that Storm—category 5 hurricane
With deafening, torrential rains

Are you trying to let life pass you by
Are you trying to have a wreck

Remain fierce
Remain focused
Remain energetic

If your life is a metaphor, this is not the one to chase
        Definitely not to succumb
slow

The Depth of Her Spirit

intense
detailed
methodical
intentional
serious

your life encompasses the elements essential to paint drying
but it is not like watching the paint dry

06/10/20

The Heart of a Woman

Glue: Strong and Invisible

Elmers.
Super.
Gorilla.
Hot.
Wood.
Rubber.
Tacky.
Stick.
Adhesive.
Epoxy.
Paste.
Thermo plastic.

Glue.
Numerous.
Various effectiveness.
Varied efficiency.

What glue joins, let no one pull apart.
Strong is the bond
Forever is the connection
Holds together through it all—
        Heat, cold, water, dry

All while unseen
Invisible

How can something invisible hold together
How does once liquid become so strong

Invisible and strong
Forever and effective

The Depth of Her Spirit

Holding and security

Glue . . .
Powerful and productive
Pensive and provocative
Profound and prolific
Long lasting and miraculous

Don't ever underestimate the ability
Of a little glue and a huge will
Be the glue that someone needs to complete
This day and face another . . .

06/10/20

The Heart of a Woman

Masked

Hid.
Veiled.
Closed.
Dark.
Darkness.
Covered.
Disguised.
Masked.

Hiding the fears
Veiling the reality
Chasing the light
Darkening the path
Darkness of the field
Covering the truth
Disguising the obvious
Masking the best parts of you

How did they become so important
To hide behind the mask?

Why wear what does not belong
To serve the psyche of someone who does not care, but desires
To suppress the authentic you?

Abandon.
Discard.
Deceive.
Dismantle.
Disgrace.
Disassemble.
Defeat.

The Depth of Her Spirit

Reject.
Reverse.
Replace.
Disclose.
Reveal.

Abandon the mask and its definition
Discard the need for the costume
Deceive those comfortable with the covering
Dismantle the mask's social status
Disgrace the pedestal—the misplaced worth
Disassemble the power of the misguided investment
Defeat those invested in that mask
Reject the approval of the mask
Reverse the misplaced respect and adoration
Replace the pretenders
Disclose the truth—escape the mask
Reveal the real you

    That the mask unsuccessfully tried to hide.

Unmask the masked.

06/10/20

The Heart of a Woman

Love Is Never Silent

Love is never silent

Love is never still

Love seldom stifles

Love is boisterous

Downright outrageous

Simply outlandish

Fully ridiculous

Love seeks

It is seeking; stalking

      Nosey and invasive

And you want to be sought out by love.

Love is unrealistic!

Deliberately offensive

Pulling innocent, and even, guilty into its

      Magnetic field of tumultuousness

Love is undefinable

Without measure

Uncontainable

Unbelievable

The Depth of Her Spirit

That annoying noise

That love makes

Demands

Requires

Bequests

Your attention

Love decapitates appetites

And destroys logic

Love seeks the fiercest

Riskiest

While requiring the softest heart for

A landing strip

Needing a watering can

And a nurturer

The fiercest

The riskiest

The boldness

    . . . love.

The most brazen of hearts grooms love,

Multiplies while duplicating,

The Heart of a Woman

Creating a safe haven

Under the most unstable environment

... for the best outcome:

A very successful love.

06/10/20

What Women Crave

Oh we crave

Oh do we crave

Your voice

Your breath

Your tone

Your touch

The way your eyes make us blush

Our cravings unresolute

Sometimes unresolved

Endless . . .

Piling up . . .

      Unsatisfied

Sometimes completely fulfilled.

Can you see the cravings

Through my thoughts

Written all over my face

Oh how we crave

Your blushing

The Heart of a Woman

Your voice

Your massage

Your pensive eyes

Your seductive glances

Your persuasive words

Your penetration

Your tenderness

Your tension

Your needs

Your responsiveness

Oh those hungry, consuming cravings

Oh these insurmountable cravings

If only you could solve the ultimate craving

The ultimate craving

The fairytale craving

The perpetual, elusive craving

Your mind
                Your life

Your heart

The Depth of Her Spirit

                Your commitment

Your self

                Your honor

Your soul

                Your thoughts

These craziest craving

One that may eternally elude

Your love

You.

Oh how do we crave

—all of you.

06/10/30

The Heart of a Woman

What Do You Know . . .

Do you know who my favorite author is and why

What about my favorite color

My favorite food

My vacation spots—favorites and most hated

You would benefit from my go-to's

My thoughts

My fears

My desires

And dreams

This road map

To know me

To understand me

To see through me

Did you know that I inadvertently made you responsible

For a significant contribution to my happiness?

And why?

Do you know that I need a reason to clean my room and balance my checkbook?

The Depth of Her Spirit

Think of the roller coasters and

The straights

Consider the nuances

And the mysteries

The details

Difficulties

So that you will understand me

When I speak

When I sleep

Drive

Roller skate

And sing

Eat

Shop

Swim

Then exercise

When I hope

And cry

When I smile

And giggle

The Heart of a Woman

What do you know

It's mostly because of you

Some of what I do is

Just because of you.

06/06/20

Seasons

There is a time to love

And to forgive

A time period to achieve

Or to fail

The time to overcome and

To persevere

A season

Or several

To love

Like

Survive

Share

To overcome

Overhaul

To commit

To console

Compromise

Seasons last a while

Or only a little while

The Heart of a Woman

There is a time to stall

Or to advance

To reflect

To refine

To start

To chase

To create

To end

To create

To end

The invest

To divest

Seasons

    Positioned to change

    Postured to challenge

    Posted to created

    Poised to charm

There is a time

That time it now.

Love

The Depth of Her Spirit

Live

Life

Do it all like your season ends now

It has no limits

But it is not unlimited

Treat that season with respect.

06/06/20

The Heart of a Woman

What I Know Now

You lose what you want

You can't deal with what you have

You are never thankful for what you got

You are always looking for something new to pursue

That is what love is all about I learned

06/06/20

The Depth of Her Spirit

On the Other Side of the Storm

The storm contains continuous, contagious conflict
Before the storm, life seems grand
    And very well may be—
    No storm in sight.
Proper preparation prevents poor storm performance
While there's no storm—prepare
Be storm ready.

Storms will come whenever they wish
Storms stay as long as they like
Storms do as much damage as they choose
Then they stop
    Spinning
    Moving
    Causing damage
        Destruction
        Pain

Survived!
On the other side of that disaster:
    Survival
    Growth
    Freedom

The Heart of a Woman

    Renewal
    Glamour
    Re—birth
    Resurrection
    Healing
    Wisdom
    Knowledge
    Strength
    Self—esteem
    Self—worth

On the other side of that storm:
    Sun
    Self—sufficiency
    Love

Wait for it
Wait for it
Wait for it
    —the other side of what has killed others,
    you have survived and lived to grow from it

05/23/20

Walked Away

He spit statements designed to
>Wilt my self-esteem

Statements designed to
>Weather my sturdy exterior

Words waging war on my
>Worth

With wonder

With worry

With wisdom
>i walked away

05/23/20

The Heart of a Woman

Hide and Seek

Qualities hidden in your mate

Seek them in the other

What a game we play with

    Another's life

When we seek to fulfill out desires

    When we are unhappy

    In the arms of another

Distanced

Shunned

Rejected

Still expecting 100% of you

How does that even happen

How did your mate miss the bullseye

    By such a huge margin

    And does not know that you

    Are not on the same target anymore

Disclose your qualities

The Depth of Her Spirit

Share your intentions

Reach transparency

    Unrelenting

    Unwavering

        Truth

Hide the deception

Delete the coy

Debate the validity of the representative

Confuse the world

Be the truth

Seek the truth

Share until it does not hurt

    Anymore . . . ever

Discard the mask

Unveil the masterpiece

    —and allow others to do the same

05/23/20

The Heart of a Woman

My Soul Mate

With complete insight
Comprehensive access
Complimentary spirits

Finishing sentences of the other
Intimate glances
Intimate conversations

Quiet walks
Romantic dinners
Reading in front of the fireplace

Intense physical attraction
World wind travel
Spontaneous visits

Endless conversation
Reading the mind of the other
Window into my soul

Access to my heart
Unlimited quest for my thoughts
Inquisitive of my nuances

The Depth of Her Spirit

Intense.

Extravagant.

Relentless.

Ridiculous.

Powerful.

Inquisitive.

Required.

Exquisite.

Spontaneous.

Specific.

Focused.

Deliberate.

Dedicated.

Committed.

My Soul Mate.

Mutual.

Outlandish.

Outrageous.

In. To. Me. See.

05/21/20

The Heart of a Woman

The Best of a Lost Love

It was good
Great even
Until it wasn't

We lost
We missed
Perseverance failed

It was good
Until we lost

But l learned
About a mystery
Known as me

Your insight into the soul
Under a fort knox security
Profound
Prolific
Pronounced
    Unimaginable vision
    Answers to questions unasked
        Unknown

The Depth of Her Spirit

Your perspective relished

Your observations researched

Your thoughts appreciated

Your intensity appreciated

Your intensity respected

    And profoundly matched

    Call and response perfected

Your strength persisted

    Held your ground through the category 5

    On dry land

    Consistent and comprehensive

Your gentleness reciprocated

    Touches

    Glances

    Dances

    Showers

The best details of our lost love

05/21/20

The Heart of a Woman

You to Me

Your struggle inspires me
Your frustration requires me
Your mishaps stop me
Your thoughts grow me
Your love motivates me

Your face lights up mine
Your words make me blush
Your hands soothe me
Your chin rests in my hair
Your kiss closes my eyes
Your hugs compels my exhale

Dreamy?
    Yes.
Gullible?
    Yes.
Stupid?
    No.

Feelings are scarce.

The Depth of Her Spirit

Authenticity is rare.

Forever is out of reach.

From you to me and back, there is hope.

You to Me.

Forever.

05/20/20

The Heart of a Woman

A Safe Place

I want to let my guard down

I want to need someone

To love someone

To have a safe, soft place to land

I just want to come home to love and warmth

Care and concern

Compassion and comfort

When the world rejects me

Listen without judgement

Questions without accusation

Love without condition

Critique without condemnation

My safe place

To help and to be helped

To learn and to become wise

To weep and to be comforted

To love and to let love

A safe place

    . . . for love

    . . . for hope

The Depth of Her Spirit

... for safety

... for my heart

Will you be my safe place?

My shelter from my storm.

05/20/20

The Heart of a Woman

Falling in Love

Deep inside my heart

This wonderful feeling glows

A feeling that I cannot resist

Dreamland overcomes me

Taking me to a paradise all his own

He has shown me a special love

One I never imagined

I want to be with him more and more

When he's around, I feel my heart soar

My heart leaps for the love he gives

 I fall for you every chance I get

By the day

By the hour

By the minute

By the second

Is there a nano second

If so, then that too.

Falling in love was easy

Staying is love is the work.

05/20/20

The Depth of Her Spirit

Closed

Sorry

. . . attraction closed for repair

The attraction created a few decades back

Unique design

One of a kind

Five star engineering

Fastest roller coaster

Tallest attraction

Well before its time

Most efficient masterpiece

Exciting attraction

Held the record for decades

Legendary experience

Phenomenal reviews

Maintains top status among competitive attractions

High maintenance

Passing time

Destructive guests

. . . all lead to damage

Fixable

But damage all the same

The Heart of a Woman

Decisive measures determined

The sign hung

Font too small to see from afar

From aways off, the attraction still appears operable

But up close

Within close range

Hardly readable

A sign explains it all

    Sorry for the inconvenience

    Attraction closed for repair!

05/20/20

The Hardest Part

I could love you
If I could just get
You to let me in.

I could love you
If I could just get
You to stop distancing me.

I could love you
If I could just get
You to draw me close.

I could love you
If I could just get
You to remember why we are made for each other.

I could love you
If I could just get
You to love me the way I love you.

That's the hardest part.

05/20/20

The Heart of a Woman

Walk in Between the Raindrops

Dance

Flip

Twirl

Strut

Stroll

Or

Walk

In between the raindrops

Silly—I know

But what else do you have to do

If you can ease the rain which chases you then

Living could start

Most of us are afraid to get wet

Not one drop should land

Raindrops

    Sad

    Breaking

    Dramatic

Raindrops

    Recoverable

The Depth of Her Spirit

    Cleansing

    Healing

Try

No excuses

Live freely

Live fully

Stop surviving

Stop getting by

And faking it

live

Live

LIVE

love

Love

LOVE

Out loud

In front of others

Because you deserve the fullness of living your dreams

The Heart of a Woman

Walk between the raindrops

Try the impossible

The absolutely unbelievable

The one thing that keeps you alive

And shaking at the same time

Do it big

Do it afraid

Do it in spite

Because of

And because it's crazy

Walk between the raindrops

And enjoy every step.

05/20/20

Tomorrow

Not one tomorrow promised

But most of them have plans

What do they hold really?

Remnants of yesterday

Or worse—the promises missed of today

Do we miss significant moments when

We plan for a hope

While missing the present

Why so important

Enjoy today

Work today

Cry today

Cherish today

Today is all that is guaranteed

Live like there is no tomorrow

Maximize today

Cherish today

The Heart of a Woman

Love like today is all that you have

Because it is

Tomorrow is a mystery

One far away

Don't leave today's worth

Until tomorrow

Don't hope tomorrow is better

Than today when you did not make sure that

Today was great.

With all of your might

Because of your wit

Focus on a today

Which makes tomorrow unnecessary.

Tomorrow.

05/20/20

Promise

I promise I love you,
I promise I do

I love you

I didn't mean to hurt you
I'm holding on to memories
Of what used to be
The relationship is not the same
No one is to blame

Once we were a
Perfect combination
Do you still love me
Will I ever have you again

The Heart of a Woman

My Black Life Matters

I survive because I am strong

I am strong because I am creative

I am creative because I believe

I believe because I am motivated

I am motivated because I am inspired

I am inspired because I am loved

I am loved because I am determined

I am determined because I am supported

I am supported because I am learning

I am learning because I am growing

I am growing because I yearn

I yearn because I am gifted

I am gifted because I am competitive

I am competitive because I am talented

I am talented because I am concerned

I am all of those things because I am black.

My Black Life Matters.

The Mirror of My Soul

Look into the mirror

You see a reflection

A reflection of self—image

Self—worth

Leaving to the naked eye only a perception

Perception based on looks alone or

Enhanced looks, whichever case is closest

This perception eventually becomes reality of an image

It is all perception

The perception of the image

The perception of the actual

Of course there is a difference

Or is it

Which one do you trust

Which one do you believe

Which one do you love

Which one is authentic

Which one love you in return

The mirror of my soul

Shares the inner most thoughts

The Heart of a Woman

Reveals the secrets

Speaks an unforeseen truth

Proceed with caution

Don't look too closely

The reality of it all is too frightening

Just take what you get

Just do what you are told, or hear

Don't try to analyze it

That mirror reveals

A loving and

Unconquerable soul

Worth the distance

Worth the trouble

And all of the effort

And definitely the love

The Depth of Her Spirit

Questions to Love

Will your words soothe my spirit and stimulate my soul

Will the touch of your hand assure me that you'll always be there

Can your mind mingle with mine and reach a resolve for the minor ailments

Will your definition of intimacy align with mine

Will your wisdom encourage my life and help restore its wellness

Consider our closeness—could a math equation draw us even closer

Reflect on our depth—will an experience keep us knitted together

Can you keep my secrets while we create our own

Can you remember my stories while we live through our own

Will you minimize my imperfections so much so that I forget that they exist

Will you love me in such an authentic manner that it feels like we have known each other 2 days past the forever that we dream of

Any more questions would lead to the love of my dreams and the man of my life.

The Heart of a Woman

The Great Mystery

. . . Love

From her first day on Creation
To the time she wrote the word
Love in his hand,
Love had been the greatest mystery.

Mystery—why?
Answers—random.

Mystery—how?
Success—rare.

From her first glance into his eyes
Until he said hello,
Love has been a unique mystery.

Mystery—when?
Questions—many.

Mystery—what?
Intimacy—exquisite.

The Depth of Her Spirit

From her first blush

Until he strolled across the room

Love has been a powerful mystery.

Love.

The great mystery.

Only began when he took her hand to dance.

A dance shares

> Power
>
> Resilience
>
> Chemistry
>
> Protection
>
> Connection
>
> Love.

From this day until forever,

Love is an essential mystery,

2020

The Heart of a Woman

Twice Dipped into That Well

Does forgiveness
Mean encountering a
Similar situation
Or even identical?

Such a profound liberation

Once.
Twice?
Twice!

Forgive
Or violently forget

Twice dipped in that well

Hurt deep
Damage irreparable
Recovery bleak

Did the outcome outweigh the risk
Did the consequence become the inconsequential
Repeat or done

The Depth of Her Spirit

How will we know

How is the risk measured

Twice dipped in that well

Stay?

Why?

Mend?

How?

Recover?

Who?

Renew?

Reconnect?

When?

Damage done

Pain experienced

Barely survived

Recovery in progress

Twice dipped in that well.

2020

The Heart of a Woman

The Perfect Words

Finding the perfect words

Escape me

Perfect ones impossible

Words meaning

Too much

Not enough

Holding the keys to forever

Able to end our relations

Keep talking

The perfect words spoken

The perfect message shared

The most perfect words

    Transparent

    Loving

    Intimate

    Protecting

    Honest

    Provocative

    Compelling

    Caring

The Depth of Her Spirit

Close

Trusting

Kind

Compassionate

The Perfect Words!

2020

The Heart of a Woman

After the Promises

After the promises of love is made
What happens next?
Promise—was it real?
Was it implied?
Did you replace actual words with
Dream words?

After the promises,
Can you keep them

After the promises,
can you deliver

after the promises,
will I love you
more or less

can I ask you for the moon
can I ask you for the stars
will you give them to me

The Depth of Her Spirit

in the form of your heart

yes, your heart.

After the promises,

What do we do

What do we have

How do we grow

How do we survive

These promises lead to love.

2020

The Heart of a Woman

With Tension

With enough tension
To feel your heart
Through my clothes
While we are both
Completely covered

Your heart beats
Through my chest

Kiss me
We are dancing

Touch me
We are talking

Hold me
We are breathing each other's breath

Hug me
We are listening to each other's thoughts

The Depth of Her Spirit

A tension

Unparalleled

Defined by chemistry

Fueled by passion

With tension, we love

The Heart of a Woman

When I Die

Will the words read 'hall of fame'

Or mystery and shame

Will the degrees be worth the toil

Or would sacrifice be foiled

When I die

Who will come

Will they cry

Because of love or

Hurt or

Hate

Will my ministry live beyond my days

Will my legacy garner your praise

Will I have made value of my days

When I inspect my life for its worth

I know You destined my for greatness since birth

I don't want to disappoint You

When we face.

when i die.

From Hello to Now

In one simple hello
And an ounce of courage
You captured my attention

From that hello to now
You listened to my cares, concerns and woes
With attentiveness and confidence

Between hello and love
You double—dutch
To invest in my life

When hello started a dialogue
While ended at dawn
While you made room for me in your life
You captured my heart

Because hello was not long enough
Because you cannot share your lifetime
In the boundaries of an afternoon
I do . . .
    For the rest of my life.

The Heart of a Woman

Dressed Up on the Outside
Naked on the Inside

She wears that designer dress well

It's sharp

Enviable

She can't believe she looks so good

The matching shoes have the audacity to be comfortable

Jazzy

Spicy

Charismatic from the ground up

The details completely in place

The accessories—matching and fabulous

The nails—perfect pink and white

The hose—ultra sheer, almost unnoticeable

Perfect

Magazine ready

Cover girl

What's underneath the suit

The Depth of Her Spirit

What exists behind the flawless foundation

Dressed up on the outside

Naked on the inside

She's broken inside

That last man broke her

Her heart shattered

Her soul neglected

Her mind infiltrated

Her needs mismanaged

Her energy drained

Her emptiness evident

Is healing forthcoming

Is love a solution

Is the negative gone yet

How can inside be rebuilt

He can the inside reflect the outside

Heart on the mend

Mind on the rebuild

Needs under new management

The Heart of a Woman

Energy revived

Soul fit to nurture

Decorate her insides

Build her esteem

Bridge the gap from the outside to the inside

Dress up the inside

She should not be naked

She is just as pretty inside as she is outside

3/2010

Shred the Memories

I was talking to a friend about an old boyfriend and she thought that I was still carrying that baggage. I find that we don't let stuff go. Letting go of the old is the only way to receive the new.

I took our pictures and shred them in her paper shredder. It felt good to know that I wouldn't see them again, although I had been afraid to let them go.

Shred the memories that force stories about the time you spent. All we really need to do is keep the lessons we learned.

That exercise forced me to release that hold. It also forced me to face the issues that I would have otherwise held on to. I wanted the relationship but not the man.

I had to let that all go when I shred the STUFF.

The Heart of a Woman

The Other Woman

Does she make you smile

Does she make you laugh

What does she do to keep your attention

The attention that I don't have

Is she pretty

Is she smart

Is she intelligent

Is she sweet

I am sure she is

I am sure that she is all of that

And then some

Does she endure the arguments

Does she persevere through the pain

Does she live in subjection to your moods

Or does she just enjoy you

Without the stuff

Without the concern of the lights

The Depth of Her Spirit

How does she deserve that time
How does she get the best of you
When I don't get the rest of you
The consistent leftovers insult me

How can I have her time
How can I be treated like the queen that I am
In the time I deserve
Not even sure how you have time to spend with her
With me in your face.

10/02/09

The Heart of a Woman

By Choice

I sleep in a twin bed

By choice

Because the king bed

Took my voice

Borrowed my independence

Challenged my heart

Disturbed my peace

By choice

So that I can retrieve my voice

Eliminating my opinion

Once so strong

Driving the force

Forcing the issues

Creating the silence

Our choices make us powerful

    Or meek

Strong

    Or weak

Amazing

The Depth of Her Spirit

    Or pitiful

I took a stand

Challenged the norms

Reconsidering my humble beginnings

Reminded of the struggles

Realizing the distance

    Between real and revised

By choice

I retrieved my voice

By choice

I retrieved myself

By choice

08/11/09

The Heart of a Woman

The Start of a Love Affair

Talking

    —long

    —intimate

    —engaging

walking

    —early

    —warm

    —natural

reading

    —together

    —sharing

    —commentary

volunteer

    —teaching

    —leading

    —journey

so when you talked to me

The Depth of Her Spirit

and encouraged me

then when you enlightened me

and invested in me

so that you could teach me

and then reach my soul

because your knowledge expanded

when I expounded on that topic

when you read that verse to me

and I cried with joy

when you shared your testimony with me

and I shared my life

then I realized I wanted you in my life

when I missed you,

a love affair was born.

01/23/09

The Heart of a Woman

Playing for Keeps

Your heart

    . . . it's mine

Your mine

    . . . it's mine

Your soul

    . . . it's mine

Your body

    . . . it's mine

Yes. I want all of you

Less than is unacceptable

Absolutely I play for keeps.

Your presence

    . . . I like it

Your time

    . . . I need it

Your thoughts

    . . . I require it

Your touch

    . . . I crave it

The Depth of Her Spirit

Yes, I need all of you.

Yes, I want you forever.

See I play for keeps.

08/09

The Heart of a Woman

Three Names Later

So who are you now

Three names later

The name originator absent

The second abusive

The third abrasive

So who are you now

Three names later

Self—esteem managed

Discipline built

Education established

Wit developed

Respect learned and earned

Even under his lack of leadership

So who are you now

Three names later

Confidence shattered

Mirror rejected

Personality challenged

Knowledge crucified

Neglect personified

Subjected to his lack of self—esteem

The Depth of Her Spirit

So who are you now

Three names later

Self—esteem wilted

Persona weakened

Vision diminished

Communication eliminated

Smile deleted

Regulated by his animalistic behavior

So who are you now

Three names later

Miraculously recovered

Authentic laughter discovered

Genuine smile refined

Self—esteem reestablished

Respect renewed

Even after his absence

Even under his abuse

Even through his abrasiveness

11/08/09

The Heart of a Woman

You are Dangerous for My Soul

It's not in your nature to nurture
It's not in your DNA to care
My soul is precious
> Too precious to chance

My soul is too precious
> Way too precious to trust
> You in ignorance
My soul avoids danger
My soul escapes danger
> At all costs
> With all my might
It's not in your heart to cherish me
It's not on your mind to put me first
My soul changes
> In your presence
> Not for the best
You tear down where you should build
Your negligence amazes me

You are dangerous for my soul
03/12/10

The Depth of Her Spirit

Hungry Can See

What Satisfied Can't

When J. California Cooper
Wrote these words
Not only did she arrest my attention
She captured my heart

She spoke to me
In such a loud voice
I couldn't hear my own breath
Or beating heart
Or was that because they both stopped

What I can see now
Yet couldn't see then
has opened my eyes
my heart
my ears
to what I had never
seen
felt
heard

The Heart of a Woman

before the hunger set in

not so long ago I was satisfied
not so long ago I was protected
      from such hunger
not so long ago I was veiled
      from my own harsh reality

Love—too much to ask?
Protection—too much to expect?
Care—too much to require?

Satisfy my wonder
Satisfy my concerns
Satisfy my needs
Satisfy my hunger

Seeking satisfied
Don't like hunger

The Depth of Her Spirit

Two Cameras

Two cameras

One color

One black and white

Leaning on that wall

Shutter opens

Flash

Image captured

Don't move

Shutten open

Flash

Captured image

Wonderful smile

Flirty glance

Simplicity defined

Two cameras

One manual

One automatic

The smile behind the camera

The Heart of a Woman

Inspired the smile in front

Two cameras
Intensity paralleled
Attraction matched

Two cameras
Dually invested
Deeply involved

Two cameras
History
Future

08/30/2009

What Makes You Stay

The tears have not stopped

They don't seem to end

He still hurts you

He still haunts you

He holds you hostage

> In your mind
>
> > With your heart
> >
> > > Through your soul

Yet you stay

Convince me of the reasonability

Of that decision

Are you will hoping

He would change

He would be more attentive

Are you still begging

For his time

For his attention

The Heart of a Woman

For his love

Are you still thinking

That something you did made him behave that way

That something you said provides him permission to mistreat you

That misbehavior can be changed

What makes you stay

When you could be loved

When you could be a whole woman

    . . . Alone.

What makes you stay.

11/02/2009

This Love, Our Love

In this season, you have become my retreat

A functional, sensual space, where being me is controversial,

But loved

Admired

Respected

And sometimes rejected

Is love enough?

For forever to be a reality?

I love you.

And always will.

The indelible impression

The forever impact

The long lasting memory

Is love enough?

For me, yes.

For you?

What do I bring to you?

What compels you to kiss my forehead?

And hold me close?

Encourage me to smother you

With all that I am

The Heart of a Woman

And what I am not?

You have taught me so much

And I have much more to learn.

I am ready.

To learn.

I have a pencil

Paper

I am attentive

I am listening

I am waiting for your instruction

I want to come to our home

Daily

To see you

To touch you

To kiss you

To hold you

You make me believe in possible

Previously impossible

I am all in.

We have gone too far to go back

No I never want to go back

I want to be one

The Depth of Her Spirit

With you

I know that I have violated some rules

Some regulations

I have ignored some warnings and some signals

I did not exercise any caution

I did not brake

I did not take a break

I am living, finally

Free to love

In the outlandish

And the outrageous way I write about

My prince charming

My rock

The best person that has ever happened to me

The Heart of a Woman

Her Worth

A woman has worth

A significant worth

Worth more than rubies

    But who even knows how much that is

A diamond, yes but even more

Pearls, yes but even more

A woman has value

Not like land or homes

Not like oil or minerals

Not even shoes

    And we know how we value those

A woman is treasure

Like ocean bottom treasure

Problem—solving treasure

Misvalued treasure

Often misunderstood

    But treasure all the same

Recognize her worth

The Depth of Her Spirit

Concede her worth

Increase her worth

Bask in her worth

Keep her worth at the forefront

      Keep her worth at the pinnacle

She is better when her worth is validated

She loves better when she feels her worth

She is worth.

The Heart of a Woman

A Homeless Heart

I want to share my heart with you

I want to give you my heart
Believing that you will take care of it
With honor, care
Love, respect
Admiration, adoration
Nurture, protection
Care for my heart better than you care for your own
Not because I am better
Not even; not ever
But because I am going to do the same
Love you to the moon and back

Oh yes because you are worth it
Protecting your heart from even my issues and
      Idiosyncrasies

So can you accept it
      Care for it
      Protect it

The Depth of Her Spirit

Hold it

Cherish it

Nurture it

So that my heart can have a home.

No longer homeless.

No longer alone.

The Heart of a Woman

Acknowledgements

God, thank You for Your plans for me. Thank You for ***The Heart of a Woman: The Depth of Her Spirit,*** and choosing me to complete Your project. I just want to please You, God. Thank You for continuing to anoint me and to invest in me and my gifts, which keep surprising me. Thank You for loving and forgiving me.

Jordan and Nehemiah, thank you for supporting me and my endeavors. Thank you for loving me, especially when I do nothing without a pen and a clipboard, thank you for enduring my late nights, your ideas, the sounding board, the love and the support. Thank you for celebrating our legacy.

To my prayer partners and to my accountability partners, thank you for the long talks and the powerful prayers and the encouragement.

To the readers who this will reach and empower and touch and affect, may these words empower you and help you reach some resolve. May you be inspired to achieve your goals and dreams. May you have courage and peace. Share love the best you can until you can share love without reservation.

The Heart of a Woman

About the Woman

As a woman who has been broken, hurt, rejected and unloved and who at some point done the breaking, hurting, rejecting, and unloving, we need to work to heal and that healing requires work. Work to heal. It is worth it to become whole.

@onediangage (twitter) ♦ onediagage@onediagage.com ♦
facebook.com/onediagageministries
youtube.com/onediagage ♦ blogtalkradio.com/onediagage ♦ ongage (instagram)
www.onediagage.com ♦ www.onediagagespeaks.com

The Heart of a Woman

ADVOCATE ♦ TEACHER ♦ FACILITATOR
CONFERENCE SPEAKER ♦ PANELIST ♦ WORKSHOP LEADER

To invite Dr. Gage to speak at your organization,

Or other group.

Please contact us at: www.onedigagespeaks.com

@onediangage (twitter) ♦ onediagage@onediagespeaks.com ♦ facebook.com/onediagage

youtube.com/onediagage ♦ blogtalkradio.com/onediagage ♦ ongage (Instagram)

The Heart of a Woman

Publishing

Do you have a book you want to write, but do not know what to do?

Do you have a book you need to publish but do not know how to start?

Would publishing move your career forward?

Let us help

onediagage@purpleink.net ♦ www.purpleink.net

713.705.5530 ♦ 281.740.5143

www.ingramcontent.com/pod-product-compliance
Lightning Source LLC
Chambersburg PA
CBHW030151100526
44592CB00009B/229